Thunderbolt's Legacy:

The Journey of A-10 Charlie

By

C.S. Duncan

Copyright © 2024 by C.S. Duncan

All rights reserved.

Prologue:

To the intrepid A-10 Thunderbolt II pilots—guardians of the battlefield and angels to the troops below—this book is dedicated to you. Flying low and fearlessly into hostile skies, you bring the fight to the enemy with unmatched precision and tenacity. You serve as the steel shield for the U.S. Army Infantry and Marine Corps, answering every call for close air support with resolute courage. Through cannon fire, smoke, and chaos, your unwavering presence is often the difference between life and death on the ground. This tribute honors your relentless dedication, battle-scarred wings, and enduring commitment to those who fight beneath you.

Greetings, everyone!

Allow me to introduce myself and share how I became part of this incredible museum. My name is A-10 Charlie, and if I close my eyes and concentrate, I can still vividly picture the moment I was brought to life.

In 1981, in the industrious town of Hagerstown, Maryland, the skilled craftsmen and engineers at Fairchild Republic assembled me with precision and purpose. I took shape under their expert hands, piece by piece, bolt by bolt. At that time, I didn't fully understand the gravity of what I was becoming. But even then, there was an undeniable sense in every rivet and every weld—that I was built for something greater.

186
A-10 Charlie
80-0186 USAF

I wasn't just a machine. I was born to protect. Designed to fly low, hit hard, and keep watch over the brave souls on the ground, my purpose stretched far beyond the metal and hydraulics that held me together. I was made for a mission forged in courage, sacrifice, and an unbreakable bond with the warfighters I would someday defend.

Over the years, I've been called many names—each representing a chapter in my story. I began as A10-535, my construction number, stamped on paper long before I left the factory floor. Then came my official designation: Military Serial Number 80-0186, United States Air Force. That number defines me to some, filed away in records and manuals. But to most, I'm better known by names that echo across battlefields: Thunderbolt II—a nod to my World War II ancestor—and perhaps most famously, Warthog.

At first, I didn't fully understand the significance these titles carried. They were just words—until I learned their meanings through the missions I flew and the warriors I supported. Over time, I realized that each name was more than a label. "Thunderbolt II" speaks to my lineage, strength, and precision. "Warthog" is spoken affectionately by those who know me best—the ground troops who count on me when danger closes in.

Each name is a part of who I am—etched into my skin, carried in the roar of my engines, and remembered in every life I've helped protect.

The Beginning

One day etched in my memory with crystal clarity: August 24th, 1981. That was the day I rolled off the assembly line—freshly painted, bolts tight, systems pristine. I gleamed under the hangar lights, every panel flush, every wire humming with potential. Though I had no battle scars or stories yet to tell, I felt a strange energy stirring. I didn't yet know what awaited me beyond those hangar doors, but I could sense it—something big, something meaningful.

The next morning—August 25th—the wait had ended.

That day, I soared into the sky for the very first time.

The sun had just begun its ascent, casting golden light across the tarmac. The air was crisp, and the sky was a boundless blue that stretched on indefinitely. I could feel the ground crew bustling around me, checking systems and preparing for launch. Everything buzzed with anticipation; within me, turbines whispered to life as if awakening from a long slumber.

Then he appeared: the test pilot.

He walked toward me with the steady stride of a man who had done this many times before. No fanfare, no theatrics. Just a quiet confidence honed by thousands of hours in the sky. As he climbed into my cockpit, I sensed a connection forming—a bond forged not by words, but by trust. We didn't need introductions. We were partners now, ready to share something extraordinary.

With a deep breath and a roar, I surged forward, my wheels lifting off the earth. In that instant, I wasn't just a machine anymore.

I was alive.

After a thorough and deliberate pre-flight inspection, everything was finally in place. The crew gave the signal. My twin General Electric TF34 engines roared to life with a deep, thunderous growl that echoed across the tarmac. I could feel the vibrations surge through my frame, every bolt and bearing humming with anticipation. Then, with a mighty howl, I lunged forward, thrust building, wheels racing along the runway.

The world blurred as I picked up speed. Faster. Louder. Stronger. The wind whipped past my frame, and when it felt like I couldn't go any quicker, the earth let go. The runway dropped away beneath me, and I rose into the air for the very first time.

Airborne.

It was more than I had ever imagined. The sky stretched endlessly before me as I surged through it with grace and raw power. The experience was exhilarating—an intoxicating mix of freedom, awe, and a flicker of uncertainty. However, that fleeting fear quickly gave way to something more profound: purpose.

In that moment, I realized:

This was where I belonged.

Not bound to the ground, but carving paths through the heavens.

I was no longer just a machine. I was alive, and the sky was my home.

Missions and Training

The next five years unfolded in a whirlwind of motion—a blur of afterburners, dog-eared flight logs, and the rhythm of relentless drills. My days shaped the next generation of A-10 pilots, soaring through the sky with eager aviators at the controls. I became their classroom in the clouds and their partner in precision. Every takeoff, maneuver, and simulated strike taught them not just how to fly but also how to survive and protect.

I was no longer just a machine made of metal, hydraulics, and circuitry. I was becoming something greater. I was evolving into a shield, a guardian, and a constant companion to the warfighters below.

Each mission revealed a new layer of my identity. I understood that my GAU-8/A Avenger cannon wasn't merely a weapon—it was my voice. That earth-shaking, unmistakable BRRRRRRRRRRT! It wasn't just the sound of firepower; it was a declaration, a warning to the enemy, and a vow to the ground troops:

You are not alone.

Help has arrived.

The sky watches over you.

With every blast from my cannon, I delivered more than just ordnance—I delivered hope.

In the beginning, uncertainty clung to me like morning fog. I had been engineered for power, precision, and war. But deep down, I couldn't help but wonder: Could I truly live up to the mission for which I was created? Would I be enough for the pilots who trusted me and climbed into my cockpit, knowing that their lives—and those they protected—rested in part on my wings?

Every mission yielded new answers.

Every flight chipped away at the doubt. I began to feel the rhythm of combat, the weight of responsibility, and the clarity of purpose. My role was simple in theory but monumental in practice: to guard the ground forces, silence threats, and carry warriors home. It was more than duty—it was identity.

But it wasn't until I saw myself through their eyes—the eyes of the troops below—that I truly began to understand what I meant. In the thunderous heartbeat of battle, they didn't see just another aircraft; they saw hope, a guardian, a promise.

Their unwavering faith in me became my strength.

And with each successful sortie, I began to understand the truth:

I was no longer just a war machine.

I was their shield, support, and silent guardian overhead.

The Battles

February 15, 1991—a day seared into my memory like afterburn on steel. The Gulf War raged on, and under the command of Colonel David A. Sawyer, I was called into action. That mission would become a defining moment in my journey—a trial by fire that tested every system, every design, and every ounce of purpose I had ever been given.

The sky was tense with the haze of conflict as we thundered low over enemy lines, my wings slicing through the desert air. We approached the target zone with precision. Then, with a sharp, calculated motion, Col. Sawyer gave the order. My bomb bay opened, and I released my payload—a spread of CBU-87 cluster bombs that tumbled earthward like silent sentinels.

Seconds later, the ground below erupted with flashes and fire. From above, I watched as each bomblet struck its target with surgical accuracy. But the mission wasn't over—not even close.

We banked hard, pulling into a tight circle. Dust and heat waves rose from the chaos below- dozens of enemy armor. Col. Sawyer's hands moved swiftly, purposefully—adjusting, tracking, locking on. I reacted as if we shared a single thought. My sensors aligned. My GAU-8 Avenger spun up, and with a deafening BRRRRRRRRT, we struck.

It wasn't just firepower—it was a symphony.

In that moment, we were one pilot and a war machine—flesh and alloy, instinct and engineering, bound by a mission and sharpened by experience. Every maneuver and shot felt effortless. We danced across the sky together, delivering protection, precision, and unrelenting force.

That day, I didn't just perform.

I proved myself.

Then, disaster struck.

Without warning, a Soviet-made SA-13 "Gopher" missile tore through the sky and slammed into my tail section, the explosion ripping through my rear fuselage with devastating force. I shuddered from nose to rudder; systems stuttered and controls felt sluggish. Warnings flashed across every panel, and my airframe trembled. For a breathless moment, I thought it might be the end.

But Col. David A. Sawyer remained composed—steady hands, calm voice, and years of experience guiding me home. Through smoke and failing systems, he wrestled me through the chaos and somehow brought me safely back to base.

I had survived, but only just.

The damage was severe. 384 puncture scars marked my body, and my tail section was mangled beyond repair. I had never felt so broken. But even then, I was not alone. The ground crew—the unsung heroes in grease-stained coveralls—were not ready to give up on me.

They devised a plan that was both daring and ingenious.

Another A-10 on the flightline had sustained catastrophic nose damage, beyond repair. However, its tail was intact. So they made a bold decision: cut the ruined rear from me and graft the healthy tail of the other A-10 onto my frame. It was aviation surgery under combat conditions—metal met metal, rivets flew, welds sparked, and within just eleven days, they had brought me back to life.

Two damaged warbirds were combined into one operational fighter.

A27

I took to the skies again—not just as a machine, but as a testament to ingenuity, resilience, and the sheer will of those who refuse to surrender. My scars became symbols of survival. My return was a defiant answer to those who attempted to take me down.

At that time, I served with the 354th Tactical Fighter Squadron, one of the most deployed units in the Air Force. Based at McChord AFB, we completed over 15,000 sorties across 11 deployments, covering Argentina, Chile, Italy, Japan, Turkey, and the Persian Gulf.

I was not just fixed.

I emerged anew—battle-forged, mission-ready, and more determined than ever.

A Period of Change

Time, as it always does, brings change.

Year after year, I watched the skies grow more crowded with sleek, newer aircraft—faster, stealthier, and brimming with next-generation technology. Their streamlined designs and cutting-edge systems offered a glimpse into the future, and I couldn't help but wonder: Was I becoming a relic of the past?

By 1998, that question appeared to find its answer when I was transferred to the Aerospace Maintenance and Regeneration Center—AMARC, the Boneyard. For many aircraft, this place marks the end of the story. However, for me, it was merely a turning point- a rebirth.

Through the Precision Engagement Modification Program, I underwent a transformation—not merely a retrofit but a complete reinvention. My analog cockpit was stripped away and replaced with sleek Multi-Function Color Displays (MFCDs), which brought clarity and control to the chaos of battle. Gone were the dials and gauges of old; in their place, vibrant screens illuminated my cockpit with data, imagery, and life-saving intel.

The addition of Hands-On Throttle and Stick (HOTAS) controls meant my pilots could manage targeting, weapons, and communication systems without ever lifting a hand off me—precision and lethality fused into instinctive motion.

But the most impactful aspect of all was my new digital data link. Suddenly, I could communicate—in real time—with ground forces, UAVs, and other aircraft. I wasn't just reacting anymore; I was part of the conversation—a node in the network—a commander's sword and a soldier's shield, sharpened for modern warfare.

I wasn't fading into irrelevance; I was charging into a new era-stronger, smarter, deadlier.

DATA LINKS

With time, I have evolved beyond my original design. I now carry advanced targeting systems such as the Sniper and LITENING pods—cutting-edge technology that provides me with the eyes of an eagle and the precision of a surgeon. These pods enable me to identify, track, and engage enemy targets with remarkable accuracy, allowing me to deploy precision-guided munitions like JDAMs (Joint Direct Attack Munitions), WCMDs (Wind-Corrected Munitions Dispensers), and laser-guided bombs with pinpoint effectiveness, even in challenging weather or combat conditions.

My internal systems also underwent a modern overhaul. Upgraded with GPS-based navigation and secure voice and data communication links, I can now integrate seamlessly into complex mission environments. These enhancements empower my crews to plan and execute operations with a level of coordination and situational awareness that once seemed unattainable.

TARGETING POD
ADOMS
NCMD
LASER GUIDE
22-280

Yet, for all these advances, I've never strayed from my roots. At my heart remains the GAU-8/A Avenger—a seven-barrel, 30mm rotary cannon capable of delivering devastating firepower against armor and fortified positions. My robust airframe, forged through years of battlefield experience, still bears the scars of countless missions, a testament to my resilience and purpose. These upgrades haven't changed who I am; they have sharpened what I was—a reliable guardian in the skies, built for the brutal demands of close air support (CAS).

The modernization program breathed new life into me. I felt a renewed energy, like an old warrior given a sharper blade and stronger armor. However, even as I soared higher and struck faster, a quiet truth began to settle in. The future was drawing closer—and with it, the inevitable realization that my time in frontline service was entering its twilight.

During this transitional phase, I was given a new name—Charlie. This name honored my legacy while recognizing the evolving role I would play in the chapters to come.

By 2013, I was stepping into a new chapter—no longer a frontline combatant, but a testbed for innovation within the Defense Advanced Research Projects Agency (DARPA). This shift was not only in mission but also in identity. My days of braving hostile skies and unleashing firepower in close air support were behind me. Now, I served a different purpose—pushing the boundaries of aerospace technology and helping to develop and evaluate systems at the very edge of possibility.

DARPA
DARPA

Gone were the urgent calls for air support and the thunder of my cannon echoing across the battlefield. In their place came quiet precision and experimentation. I was no longer forged for war but refined for discovery. Though this transformation hinted at melancholy, it was also a dignified evolution. I wasn't being retired; I was being repurposed, entrusted to shape the future by testing what tomorrow's warriors might depend on.

I understood that the role I once played in combat had left a mark on the battlefield and the history of air power itself. Although the roar of battle had faded from my ears, I embraced this new mission with resolve. The skies no longer beckoned me as they once did, yet I knew I still had something to offer. My legacy was no longer written in sorties and fire missions—it was now etched into data streams, prototypes, and lessons that would guide the next generation.

This was not an end; it was a quiet continuation, a new kind of contribution, and I accepted it with purpose.

DARPA

The Last Flight

I'll never forget the weight of that morning. The sky above was a familiar canvas—open, endless, welcoming. I had flown beneath it countless times, slicing through clouds and wind with purpose. But that day, something felt different. The air was heavier, quieter, as though even the winds understood what was about to unfold. Every movement I made felt just a fraction slower, more deliberate, as if some part of me knew—this would be my final flight.

From takeoff to touchdown, I carried myself with quiet pride. My engines roared one last time, my wings cut through the air gracefully, and I flew not for a mission, but for memory. When my wheels kissed the runway, the silence that followed was louder than any battle I had ever faced. I stopped, and the ground crew approached—not with urgency, but with solemn respect. Then, without ceremony, they began disconnecting my systems and unbolting panels, reaching deep into the heart of who I was. As the first engine came free, the reality hit: I would never fly again.

And yet, there was no sorrow in that moment- only peace.

I lived a life of purpose—through thousands of missions, I shielded allies, supported warriors, and wrote my name into the skies. I defied the odds, outlasted expectations, and stood the test of time. My journey did not end in fire or failure, but in dignity and honor.

Though the sky no longer called to me, I knew I wouldn't be forgotten. My legacy had taken flight long before this last mission—and it would continue to soar in the stories, the memories, and the lives I had helped protect.

I had fulfilled my duty; now, I could rest.

Raytheon

Piece by piece, I was carefully disassembled. What had once been a finely tuned machine of war, always ready at a moment's notice, now stood still—my systems powered down, my frame exposed to the quiet. My cockpit, once alive with movement, voices, and the hum of instruments, now rested in solemn silence. In that silence, I discovered something unexpected: peace.

My wings—those faithful extensions that had carried me into danger, across hostile skies, and through storms of steel— were now still, their mission complete. They would never rise again, never feel the rush of wind or the burn of afterburners, but that final stillness carried no sadness. Instead, there was a quiet dignity in their rest.

I had given my all. Every flight, every mission, and every moment spent in the sky had been driven by purpose and pride. I had protected, supported, and stood firm when it mattered most. My time ended, not in defeat but in fulfillment. My role in the grand story of aviation and defense was complete.

Others would now take to the skies, carrying the torch forward. Newer wings, sharper tools, and fresher eyes would continue the fight, shaped partly by the legacy I helped forge. My journey had reached its final chapter, but the pride of what I had accomplished still lingered—etched into the hangar walls, whispered through the winds, and echoing far above in the skies I once called home.

A New Home

Just when I believed my journey had quietly ended, something unexpected happened in 2016. After years of standing exposed beneath open skies—my paint faded, my panels kissed by rain and sun—I was gently moved to a new resting place: the Evergreen Aviation & Space Museum in McMinnville, Oregon.

For a time, I feared I had been forgotten, my legacy left to rust with the passage of time. But I was wrong. I hadn't been abandoned; I had been chosen. My story still had a role to fulfill

A New Purpose

At the museum, I was in the hands of a dedicated team of restoration specialists—craftsmen and caretakers of history. To the untrained eye, I might have appeared to be little more than a weathered relic, my surfaces dulled by time, my joints stiff with disuse. But to them, I was something more significant. They didn't just see corroded metal or faded paint—they saw a legacy. They saw a story worth preserving.

With care and precision, they began their work. They stripped away years of grime and rust, revealing the battles I had survived and the journeys I had endured. Each brushstroke of fresh camouflage paint, each bolt tightened and panel realigned, stood as a tribute to what I had once been. When they reinstalled my mock GAU-8/A Avenger cannon, it was not merely a weapon but a symbol of the power I had once wielded and the protection I had offered.

Within the museum walls, surrounded by legends of flight and feats of space exploration, I discovered a new kind of purpose. I was no longer called to combat or sky patrols; instead, I stood ready—this time, as a teacher. As a symbol. As a bridge between generations.

Visitors now walk beneath my wings, their eyes wide with wonder. Children press their hands against the glass, imagining what it felt like to fly with me. Veterans stop in silence, recalling their stories as they stand before me. And through it all, my spirit soars again—not in altitude, but in impact.

I may never leave the ground again, but I am far from grounded. My story is being told, and my purpose is renewed. In this place of honor and remembrance, I've discovered that even after the final flight, the mission can still continue.

A-10 201

I recognized something profound in their reverent touch: my mission had changed.

I was no longer a warfighter destined for combat; I had become a storyteller. Every scratch they chose to preserve, every dent left untouched, told a tale of purpose, courage, and resilience. I was now a voice for those who once flew me, maintained me, and trusted me with their lives.

Now, I stand not as a machine of war, but as a monument to perseverance and sacrifice. My airframe no longer climbs into the sky, but my story soars higher than ever, etched into the minds of those who walk by, their eyes wide with curiosity and their hearts stirred by the echoes of my past.

I am no longer a weapon; I am a witness to history.

A-10

Now, I am surrounded not by the roar of engines or the urgency of war, but by the quiet footsteps of curious visitors. Children stand before me, eyes wide with wonder, their small fingers pointing eagerly as they imagine the roar of my engines and the thrill of flight. They ask questions with innocent awe— "Did you fly in a war?" "Were you ever scared?" "What was it like up there?" In their voices, I hear the echoes of the future—young minds ignited by the past.

Then come the veterans. They approach not with excitement but with reverence. Some stand silently, hands behind their backs, offering me a subtle nod—a gesture heavy with understanding. Others linger a little longer, their eyes scanning every rivet and panel, memories flickering across their faces like old film reels. In their silence, I feel the weight of shared experiences, of lives once intertwined with mine in the crucible of service.

In these moments, I recognize my new mission.

I am no longer just a machine of war. I am a keeper of memory, a voice for those who can no longer speak, and a spark for those who are just beginning to dream. I stand here not merely as an aircraft but as a symbol—of courage, sacrifice, and resilience. My presence reminds each visitor that history is not just something written in books; it is something felt, lived, and carried forward.

Through each child's question and every veteran's silent tribute, I persist in serving—not by flying, but by inspiring. My mission endures in the hearts I touch and the stories I help to tell.

A-10
WARTHOGHOG

A Final Mission

Though I no longer slice through the clouds or thunder across distant skies, my purpose endures. I may be grounded, my engines silent, but I am not finished—not by a long shot.

Now, I stand proudly on display, not as a relic of the past, but as a living symbol of service and sacrifice. My mission has transformed. No longer tasked with combat or reconnaissance, I now serve as a beacon of remembrance. I inspire the young, honor the brave, and remind all who stand before me that duty, courage, and perseverance never go out of style.

Every rivet in my frame, every scar etched into my skin, speaks of the battles I've faced and the lives I've protected. I am a chapter of history cast in aluminum and steel—a testament to those who flew, fought, and fell alongside me.

Though I no longer fly, my spirit soars in the hearts of those who remember. Veterans recall their comrades. Children dream of flight. Generations yet to come will walk past, pause, and feel the weight of my story.

This is my final mission: to ensure that what I stand for never fades and that my legacy continues to soar—high and proud—on the wings of memory.

I am the A-10C Thunderbolt II, known as the Warthog—or simply Charlie to my friends. Though my days soaring through the skies are behind me, I have found peace in knowing that I served with honor and purpose. Now, in this museum, surrounded by the rich history of aviation and the eager faces of future generations, I continue to serve in a different way—by telling my story. My legacy lives on through those who listen and remember.

Lesser-known facts about the A-10 Thunderbolt II, also known as the "Warthog":

1. Survivability and Redundancy: The A-10 is designed to survive heavy damage. Its cockpit is surrounded by a titanium "bathtub" that can withstand direct hits from armor-piercing and high-explosive projectiles up to 23mm. Thanks to redundant systems, the aircraft can fly with half a wing, one engine, no tail, or missing control surfaces.

2. Designed Around the GAU-8 Cannon: The A-10 was essentially built around its primary weapon, the 30mm GAU-8/A Avenger rotary cannon. The massive cannon fires armor-piercing depleted uranium rounds at a rate of up to 3,900 rounds per minute. Its size necessitated a slight offset of the A-10's landing gear to accommodate it within the aircraft's structure.

3. The aircraft's nose gear: The nose gear is positioned to the left of the centerline to accommodate the GAU-8.

4. Slow and Steady: Unlike many modern aircraft, the A-10 is not a fast jet. Its relatively slow speed (maximum of about 420 mph) enables it to loiter over the battlefield for extended periods, allowing for precision close air support.

5. Engine Placement: The A-10's engines are mounted high above the fuselage, an unusual design choice intended to protect them from ground fire and debris kicked up during low-level flights. This configuration also allows the engines to operate more efficiently under damaged conditions, providing thrust even when hit.

Lesser-known facts about the A-10 Thunderbolt II, also known as the "Warthog" Con't

6. Reversible Flight Controls: The A-10 features mechanical backup systems for its flight controls. If the hydraulic systems are damaged, the pilot can still fly the aircraft using manual inputs. This provides an added layer of survivability and distinguishes it among modern fighter jets.

7. Low-Maintenance: The A-10 was designed to operate in austere conditions and has low maintenance requirements. Its simple construction and rugged design enable servicing in the field with minimal resources, making it an ideal aircraft for forward operations.

8. Battle-Damaged Record: In the Gulf War and subsequent conflicts, several A-10s returned to base despite sustaining heavy damage, including hits that would have downed most other aircraft. One notable case involved an A-10 returning with one engine, one wing almost completely torn off, and severe structural damage, showcasing its extreme resilience.

9. Psychological Impact: The A-10's low-altitude presence and the distinctive sound of its cannon have a significant psychological effect on enemy ground forces. The GAU-8's "brrrrt" is so intimidating that many adversaries retreat or surrender upon hearing it approach.

10. Armored Cockpit Design: The titanium cockpit armor, often referred to as the "bathtub," weighs over 1,200 pounds and provides high levels of protection to the pilot. It is designed to shield the pilot from small arms fire and shrapnel, further enhancing the Warthog's reputation for survivability.

Lesser-known facts about the A-10 Thunderbolt II, also known as the "Warthog" Con't

11. Decades of Service: Despite its development in the 1970s, the A-10 has consistently proven itself in modern combat environments. Efforts to retire the A-10 in favor of more advanced jets have repeatedly been delayed or canceled due to its irreplaceable role in close air support.

12. Versatility in Ammunition: The A-10's GAU-8/A Avenger cannon can fire various types of rounds, including high-explosive incendiary and armor-piercing incendiary (API) rounds. These rounds are effective against both soft targets, such as infantry and light vehicles, and hardened targets, like tanks.

13. GAU 8/A Accuracy: the main gun can accurately engage targets up to 6,500 meters, equivalent to 59 football fields or 4.04 miles.

14. Only one barrel is firing: The main gun is offset from the center line of the aircraft. Therefore, the barrel at the seven o'clock position fires as it rotates, maintaining its aim down the center line of the plane.

15. Short Takeoff and Landing: The A-10 can take off and land on rough, short airstrips, making it ideal for close support operations from forward locations. This capability allows it to be deployed closer to battlefields, thereby reducing response time for troops in need of air support.

Lesser-known facts about the A-10 Thunderbolt II, also known as the "Warthog" Con't

16. Wings Designed for Maneuverability: The A-10's straight-wing design offers excellent low-speed Maneuverability and stable flight characteristics, making it ideal for the ground-attack role, especially in close air support missions where precision and agility are critical.

17. Long Loiter Time: The A-10's fuel-efficient turbofan engines enable it to loiter over battle zones for extended periods, which is a significant advantage when delivering persistent close air support to ground forces.

18. The A-10 Thunderbolt II performs a "bump maneuver": This is done to enhance targeting and weapon delivery accuracy during attack runs, particularly when using unguided munitions such as the A-10's 30mm GAU-8/A Avenger cannon or bombs. This maneuver consists of a rapid climb followed by a roll and dive toward the target.

19. International Usage: While primarily utilized by the United States, the A-10 has attracted interest from other countries. Although no foreign sales have taken place, several allied nations have explored or requested its capabilities for similar close-air-support missions.

About the Author

Clemons S. Duncan is a distinguished author and aviation expert with an impressive 24-year career in the U.S. Army. During this time, he served as a helicopter pilot, trained for all special operations missions. His expertise extends beyond the cockpit; he later became the lead Aircraft Accident Investigator for the Naval Air Systems Command (NAVAIR). His career has been marked by excellence, as demonstrated by multiple awards, including the Meritorious Service Medal, Air Medal, and Senior Army Aviator Badge.

In addition to his military service, Clemons has utilized his extensive knowledge to make significant contributions to aviation safety and education. As a Certified Lean Six Sigma Master Black Belt, he has led innovative process improvement initiatives and taught graduate and undergraduate courses in aeronautics, safety, and accident investigation at Embry-Riddle Aeronautical University. Clemons is the author of numerous books on aviation, combining technical expertise with a passion for storytelling to engage and inform readers about the dynamic world of flight and safety.